5 STEPS TO UNSHAKEABLE CONFIDENCE

5 Steps to Unshakeable Confidence

Unlock Your Inner Power

B. VINCENT

QuantumQuill Press

CONTENTS

| 1 |

Chapter 1: Understanding Confidence

Defining Confidence:

Confidence is greater than simply a feeling; it is a critical factor of our being that shapes how we pick out ourselves and engage with the world round us. In its essence, self assurance is the unwavering faith in oneself, the assurance that we possess the competencies and traits wished to navigate life's challenges and pursue our desires with conviction.

To in reality apprehend confidence, we need to delve past surface definitions and discover its multifaceted nature. It encompasses now not solely self-assurance however additionally resilience, assertiveness, and a high-quality self-image. Confidence is the gasoline that propels us forward, enabling us to include opportunities, overcome obstacles, and thrive in the face of adversity.

In this chapter, we embark on a trip to unravel the complexities of confidence, inspecting its roots in psychology, its have an impact on behavior, and its function in shaping our lives. By gaining a deeper grasp of what self belief really entails, we lay the basis for cultivating unshakeable self-assurance and unlocking our internal power.

Through insightful anecdotes, professional insights, and sensible exercises, we will discover the a range of dimensions of confidence, empowering readers to redefine their relationship with themselves and the world round them. Together, we will embark on a transformative experience towards self-discovery, as we discover the key standards and practices that structure the bedrock of unshakeable confidence.

The Psychology of Confidence:

Confidence is no longer purely a state of mind; it is deeply rooted in the difficult workings of the human psyche. Understanding the psychology in the back of self belief unveils the mechanisms with the aid of which our thoughts, beliefs, and experiences form our self-perception and behavior.

At its core, self belief is constructed upon a basis of self-esteem, which encompasses our feel of self esteem and value. It is influenced by means of a myriad of factors, together with previous experiences, social interactions, and cultural norms. From early childhood improvement to adulthood, our self belief undergoes a non-stop evolution, fashioned by using the remarks we get hold of from others and the way we interpret and internalize these messages.

Central to the psychology of self belief is the thought of self-efficacy, coined by means of psychologist Albert Bandura. Self-efficacy refers to our trust in our capability to attain precise desires and tasks. When we have excessive self-efficacy, we strategy challenges with optimism and perseverance, viewing disasters as possibilities for boom instead than setbacks.

Moreover, our ideas and beliefs play a pivotal function in shaping our self assurance levels. Negative self-talk and limiting beliefs can undermine our self-assurance, whereas high-quality affirmations and cognitive restructuring strategies can empower us to domesticate a extra resilient mindset.

By delving into the psychology of confidence, we acquire precious insights into the internal workings of our minds and the elements that have an effect on our feel of self-assurance. Armed with this knowledge, we are higher outfitted to perceive and assignment the bad concept patterns and beliefs that keep us back, paving the way for a extra assured and gratifying life.

Common Misconceptions:

In our pursuit of confidence, we frequently come upon misconceptions and myths that cloud our grasp of what it simply skill to be confident. These misconceptions can lead us astray, inflicting us to undertake dangerous beliefs and behaviors that undermine our shallowness and avert our growth.

One frequent misconception about self assurance is that it is synonymous with vanity or overconfidence. However, real self belief is rooted in humility and self-awareness, as an alternative than an inflated feel of superiority. It is about acknowledging our strengths and boundaries with grace and authenticity, as a substitute than looking for validation or approval from others.

Another common delusion is that self belief is some thing we both have or don't have, a constant trait that can't be developed or cultivated. In reality, self belief is a talent that can be realized and honed via exercise and perseverance. By adopting a boom attitude and embracing failure as section of the studying process, we can steadily construct our self belief over time.

Additionally, there is a false impression that self belief skill in no way feeling concern or doubt. In truth, even the most assured people trip moments of uncertainty and vulnerability. What units them aside is their capacity to renowned and confront their fears, instead than permitting them to dictate their actions.

By debunking these frequent misconceptions, we free ourselves from the constraints of limiting beliefs and open ourselves up to new possibilities. We apprehend that self belief is no longer about conforming to societal expectations or measuring ourselves towards exterior standards, however as an alternative about embracing our proper selves and proudly owning our worthiness. In doing so, we pave the way for a deeper, extra profound feel of self belief that emanates from within.

The Benefits of Confidence:

Confidence is now not simply a ideal trait; it is a effective catalyst for private and expert success. When we possess unshakeable confidence, we are extra probable to pursue our dreams with determination, resilience, and a experience of purpose. The advantages of self belief prolong a long way past mere self-assurance, permeating each and every component of our lives and shaping our experiences in profound ways.

One of the most big advantages of self belief is its affect on our intellectual and emotional well-being. When we accept as true with in ourselves and our abilities, we ride decrease stages of stress, anxiety, and self-doubt. We are higher geared up to deal with challenges and setbacks, viewing them as possibilities for boom alternatively than insurmountable obstacles.

Confidence additionally performs a critical function in our interpersonal relationships. When we exude confidence, we are greater probable to entice fantastic humans and possibilities into our lives. We talk assertively, set boundaries effectively, and domesticate deeper connections with others primarily based on mutual admire and admiration.

Moreover, self assurance is intently linked to expert success and profession advancement. Studies have proven that assured people are greater probable to take on management roles, negotiate greater salaries, and reap larger ranges of job satisfaction. They are viewed as credible, competent, and successful of tackling complicated challenges with poise and assurance.

Beyond the tangible benefits, self belief additionally fosters a feel of empowerment and fulfillment. When we accept as true with in ourselves, we method existence with a experience of optimism and enthusiasm, keen to embody new experiences and capture possibilities for growth. We turn out to be the architects of our personal destiny, charting a path towards a brighter, greater gratifying future.

By recognizing the myriad advantages of confidence, we are stimulated to domesticate this worthwhile trait inside ourselves. Through self-reflection, self-awareness, and intentional action, we can unencumber our internal energy and unleash our full potential, assured in our potential to create the existence we desire.

Assessing Your Current Confidence Level:

Before embarking on the experience to domesticate unshakeable confidence, it is fundamental to take inventory of where you presently stand. Self-awareness is the cornerstone of private growth, and assessing your modern-day self assurance degree offers precious insights into areas of power and areas for improvement.

Begin by way of reflecting on your previous experiences and how they have formed your confidence. Consider moments when you felt most assured and empowered, as nicely as instances when you struggled with self-doubt and insecurity. What patterns emerge? Are there unique conditions or triggers that affect your self assurance positively or negatively?

Next, take stock of your beliefs and thinking patterns surrounding confidence. Are there any limiting beliefs or bad self-talk that keep you returned from wholly embracing your potential? Challenge these beliefs by way of analyzing the proof helping them and reframing them in a extra empowering light.

Practical self-assessment equipment can additionally be beneficial in gauging your modern-day self assurance level. Consider finishing workouts such as self-confidence surveys or confidence-building things to do to reap a clearer appreciation of your strengths and areas for growth.

Finally, are trying to find comments from depended on friends, household members, or mentors who can provide precious insights into your strengths and areas for improvement. Be open to optimistic criticism and use it as an probability for increase as an alternative than taking it personally.

By assessing your cutting-edge self belief stage with honesty and self-awareness, you lay the groundwork for significant trade and transformation. Armed with this knowledge, you are higher geared up to perceive areas of center of attention and tailor your strategy to constructing unshakeable self assurance that radiates from within.

| 2 |

Chapter 2: Cultivating a Positive Mindset

Recognizing Negative Thought Patterns:

Our ideas have a effective affect on our emotions, behaviors, and ultimately, our degree of confidence. In this section, we will delve into the frequent bad thinking patterns that frequently lurk under the surface, sabotaging our shallowness and undermining our feel of worth.

Negative concept patterns can take more than a few forms, from self-criticism and self-doubt to catastrophizing and all-or-nothing thinking. These patterns can emerge as so ingrained in our minds that we may also no longer even be conscious of their presence or their have an impact on our lives.

By studying to apprehend these poor concept patterns, we can commence to project and reframe them, changing them with greater positive and empowering beliefs. This procedure requires self-awareness and a willingness to study our ideas with honesty and curiosity.

One frequent terrible notion sample is the internal critic, that voice of self-doubt and self-criticism that whispers regularly in our minds, telling us we're no longer exact ample or successful enough. Another is the tendency to catastrophize, imagining the worst-case eventualities and magnifying our fears and anxieties out of proportion.

By shining a mild on these bad notion patterns, we can start to see them for what they are: mere illusions created through our minds. We can assignment their validity and substitute them with greater rational and compassionate ideas that aid our self assurance and well-being.

Through mindfulness practices such as meditation and journaling, we can domesticate increased focus of our ideas and study to examine them with detachment, as an alternative than turning into entangled in their grip. With exercise and patience, we can progressively rewire our brains for positivity and confidence, releasing ourselves from the shackles of poor questioning and stepping into our full potential.

The Power of Affirmations:

Affirmations are a effective device for reshaping our attitude and cultivating unshakeable confidence. At their core, affirmations are tremendous statements that we repeat to ourselves regularly, with the intention of instilling beliefs that aid our dreams and aspirations.

The electricity of affirmations lies in their potential to reprogram the unconscious mind, which governs plenty of our thoughts, beliefs, and behaviors. By constantly reinforcing effective messages, we can overwrite old, limiting beliefs and exchange them with new, empowering ones.

When crafting affirmations, it is fundamental to pick phrases that resonate deeply with us and replicate the truth we want to create. Rather than the use of indistinct or established statements, such as "I am confident," we can be extra unique and intentional, focusing on traits and consequences we simply desire.

For example, rather of saying, "I am confident," we would possibly say, "I exude self belief in each thing of my life," or "I have confidence in my capabilities to overcome challenges and gain my goals." These statements are no longer solely extra particular however additionally greater emotionally resonant, evoking a experience of conviction and belief.

To maximize the effectiveness of affirmations, it is critical to include them into our each day movements consistently. Whether thru day by day affirmations rituals, written affirmations, or spoken affirmations, the key is repetition and consistency.

Over time, as we proceed to beef up these fantastic messages, they start to take root in our unconscious mind, influencing our thoughts, beliefs, and ultimately, our actions. We locate ourselves embodying the characteristics and traits we affirm, stepping into a fact the place self belief flows without difficulty and abundantly.

Incorporating affirmations into our each day exercise is no longer about denying or suppressing terrible thoughts; rather, it is about consciously deciding on to center of attention our interest on what we prefer to create in our lives. It's a effective act of self-love and self-empowerment, reminding ourselves of our inherent well worth and potential.

By harnessing the strength of affirmations, we can faucet into the limitless reservoir of self assurance that resides inside us, unlocking our internal electricity and embracing a existence crammed with purpose, passion, and possibility.

Practicing Gratitude:

In the pursuit of cultivating a fine mind-set and fostering unshakeable confidence, the exercise of gratitude emerges as a transformative tool. Gratitude is the exercise of acknowledging and appreciating the abundance and advantages existing in our lives, no count number how small or apparently insignificant they can also be.

At its core, gratitude is a mindset—a way of viewing the world thru a lens of abundance and understanding instead than shortage and lack. When we domesticate a spirit of gratitude, we shift our focal point from what we lack to what we have, from what's incorrect to what's right, from what's lacking to what's present.

Research in high quality psychology has persistently proven that working towards gratitude is related with several advantages for intellectual and emotional well-being. Regular gratitude exercise has been linked to multiplied emotions of happiness, satisfaction, and universal existence fulfillment. It can additionally limit signs of melancholy and anxiousness and enhance resilience in the face of adversity.

There are many methods to contain gratitude into our each day lives, from retaining a gratitude journal to working towards mindfulness and gratitude meditation. The key is to discover practices that resonate with us in my opinion and make them a steady section of our routine.

Each day, take a few moments to replicate on the matters you are grateful for, whether or not it is the love and assist of buddies and family, the splendor of nature, or the easy pleasures of each day life. Cultivate an mindset of grasp for each the huge benefits and the small joys that encompass you.

By practicing gratitude regularly, we instruct our minds to center of attention on the fantastic components of our lives, fostering a feel of abundance and contentment that permeates each element of our being. We emerge as greater resilient in the face of challenges, extra compassionate towards ourselves and others, and greater attuned to the richness and splendor of the existing moment.

Ultimately, gratitude is now not simply a fleeting emotion or brief nation of mind; it is a way of being—a way of dwelling our lives with open hearts and minds, and a deep grasp for the treasured present of existence. As we domesticate gratitude in our lives, we nourish our souls and domesticate the fertile soil in which unshakeable self assurance can take root and flourish.

Visualization Techniques:

Visualization is a effective device for constructing self assurance and manifesting our desires. It entails mentally picturing ourselves reaching our dreams and embodying the traits we desire to cultivate. Through visualization, we harness the innovative energy of the idea to form our fact and carry our aspirations to life.

The exercise of visualization faucets into the brain's ability to simulate experiences and create new neural pathways. When we vividly think about ourselves succeeding, our talent interprets these intellectual pictures as actual experiences, activating the equal neural networks related with authentic performance. As a result, we support the neural connections related with self assurance and competence, reinforcing our faith in our potential to obtain our goals.

To start training visualization, locate a quiet and relaxed area the place you can loosen up and focal point your attention. Close your eyes and take quite a few deep breaths to middle your self and quiet your mind. Then, think about your self in a scenario the place you sense assured and empowered. Visualize the scene in vivid detail, enticing all of your senses to make the ride as actual and immersive as possible.

As you visualize your self succeeding, pay interest to how it feels in your body. Notice the sensations of self assurance and empowerment coursing via you, filling you with a feel of energy and resilience. Allow your self to thoroughly embody the characteristics you desire to cultivate, embracing the model of your self who is confident, capable, and unstoppable.

It's integral to exercise visualization commonly to reap its full benefits. Set apart devoted time every day to have interaction in visualization exercises, ideally incorporating them into your morning or bedtime pursuits for most effectiveness. The greater constantly you practice, the extra deeply ingrained the high quality intellectual imagery turns into in your unconscious mind.

In addition to visualizing success, you can additionally use visualization to rehearse difficult conditions and mentally put together your self to cope with them with self belief and grace. By visualizing your self overcoming barriers and navigating difficulties with ease, you construct resilience and give a boost to your self belief in the face of adversity.

As you proceed to exercise visualization, you will word a profound shift in your mind-set and behavior. You will grow to be extra attuned to the possibilities and chances that encompass you, and greater assured in your capability to create the lifestyles you desire. Visualization turns into now not simply a method however a way of life—a effective device for shaping your fact and unlocking your full potential.

Building Resilience:

Resilience is the secret weapon of these who exude unshakeable confidence. It is the capacity to leap returned from setbacks, adapt to change, and thrive in the face of adversity. Building resilience is imperative for cultivating a nice attitude and weathering the inevitable challenges that existence throws our way.

At its core, resilience is no longer about keeping off failure or adversity; it is about how we reply to them. Resilient persons view setbacks as possibilities for boom and learning, as a substitute than insurmountable obstacles. They embody failure as a herbal section of the ride towards success and continue to be steadfast in their faith in their capacity to overcome challenges.

There are numerous techniques for constructing resilience and strengthening our potential to leap lower back from adversity. One key thing is cultivating a increase mindset, which entails reframing setbacks as possibilities for increase and viewing challenges as mastering experiences. By adopting a boom mindset, we turn out to be greater bendy and adaptable, in a position to pivot and modify path when confronted with obstacles.

Another essential thing of resilience is growing a sturdy guide community of friends, family, and mentors who can furnish encouragement, guidance, and standpoint all through tough times. Having a aid device in vicinity can assist us sense much less by myself and greater resilient in the face of adversity.

Practicing self-care is additionally quintessential for constructing resilience and keeping ordinary well-being. Taking care of our physical, emotional, and intellectual fitness helps us recharge our batteries and fill up our reserves of resilience. This can contain things to do such as exercise, meditation, spending time in nature, and attractive in pursuits and pastimes that carry us pleasure and fulfillment.

Finally, cultivating gratitude and focusing on the advantageous factors of our lives can bolster our resilience and assist us keep a fine outlook, even in difficult times. By acknowledging and appreciating the advantages and possibilities that encompass us, we domesticate a feel of resilience and internal electricity that permits us to navigate life's ups and downs with grace and confidence.

By incorporating these techniques into our each day lives, we can domesticate resilience and reinforce our self belief in the face of adversity. We emerge as extra adept at bouncing lower back from setbacks, greater adaptable in the face of change, and extra assured in our capacity to overcome something challenges lifestyles may additionally throw our way. Building resilience is no longer simply about surviving; it is about thriving, and embracing the ride with courage, determination, and unshakeable confidence.

| 3 |

Chapter 3: Embracing Self-Acceptance

Grasping Self-Acknowledgment:

Self-acknowledgment is the foundation of certainty and prosperity, yet it is many times misjudged or disregarded as we continued looking for personal growth. At its embodiment, self-acknowledgment is tied in with embracing ourselves completely and genuinely, blemishes what not. It is the readiness to recognize and embrace each part of what our identity is — the upside, the awful, and the blemished.

To really comprehend self-acknowledgment, we should initially perceive that it isn't inseparable from smugness or renunciation. It doesn't imply that we are happy with our ongoing conditions or that we want development and improvement. All things considered, it is tied in with burying the hatchet with ourselves as we are at this time, while likewise endeavoring to turn into our best selves.

Self-acknowledgment starts with mindfulness — the capacity to perceive and recognize our contemplations, sentiments, and ways of behaving without judgment or analysis. It expects us to develop a caring and nonjudgmental disposition toward ourselves, treating ourselves with the very consideration and understanding that we would propose to a dear companion.

One of the greatest boundaries to self-acknowledgment is the internal pundit — the voice of self-uncertainty and self-analysis that subverts our certainty and confidence. By figuring out how to quiet the inward pundit and develop self-sympathy, we make space for self-acknowledgment to thrive.

Self-acknowledgment likewise includes relinquishing the requirement for outer approval and endorsement. Rather than looking for approval from others, we figure out how to approve ourselves — to perceive our value and innate worth free of outer awards or accomplishments.

Eventually, self-acknowledgment is an excursion — a constant course of self-revelation, development, and confidence. It requires boldness, weakness, and a readiness to embrace our mankind in the entirety of its untidy, wonderful intricacy. As we set out on this excursion of self-acknowledgment, we establish the groundwork for unshakeable certainty and internal harmony, realizing that we are enough similarly as we are.

Conquering Self-Uncertainty:

Self-question is a typical hindrance on the way to self-acknowledgment and certainty. It appears as that pestering voice in our minds that questions our capacities, subverts our value, and fills us with vulnerability and frailty. Conquering self-question expects us to challenge the legitimacy of these negative contemplations and convictions, and to develop a more profound identity confirmation and self-trust.

Perhaps the earliest move toward defeating self-question is to see the truth about it — a silly apprehension established in previous encounters, restricting convictions, and cultural molding. By recognizing that self-question did not depend on true reality but instead on our discernments and translations of the real world, we can start to release its hold on our psyches.

Then, we can deal with reexamining our negative considerations and convictions into more sure and enabling ones. This includes testing the exactness and legitimacy of our self-uncertainty and supplanting it with more reasonable and merciful self-talk. Rather than harping on our apparent inadequacies and disappointments, we can zero in on our assets, achievements, and potential for development.

Rehearsing self-empathy is one more remarkable cure to self-question. By treating ourselves with graciousness, understanding, and pardoning, we establish a supporting inward climate where self-question battles to flourish. We can offer ourselves the very love and backing that we would propose to a dear companion confronting comparative questions and instabilities.

Besides, making a move disregarding our self-question is vital to building certainty and self-trust. At the point when we propel ourselves beyond our usual ranges of familiarity and face challenges, we demonstrate to ourselves that we are skilled and strong, no matter what our feelings of trepidation and vulnerabilities. Every little step we steer toward our objectives fortifies our certainty and decreases the force of self-question.

At long last, looking for help from others can be instrumental in conquering self-question. Whether through treatment, instructing, or support gatherings, having a place of refuge to investigate our questions and fears can give important viewpoint and consolation. Encircling ourselves with individuals who have faith in us and backing our development can assist us with building the certainty and flexibility expected to conquer self-uncertainty and embrace self-acknowledgment.

Observing Your Assets:

Integral to the excursion of self-acknowledgment is the acknowledgment and festivity of our interesting assets and gifts. Again and again, we center around our apparent imperfections and deficiencies, disregarding the many gifts and capacities that make us what our identity is. By moving our thoughtfulness regarding our assets, we support our confidence as well as develop a more profound identity acknowledgment and appreciation for ourselves.

Distinguishing our assets starts with self-reflection and mindfulness. Carve out opportunity to ponder the exercises, abilities, and characteristics that easily fall into place for you and give you pleasure. Consider the commendations and criticism you have gotten from others, as they can frequently give significant experiences into your assets.

Whenever you have distinguished your assets, put forth a cognizant attempt to celebrate and support them. Recognize your achievements and accomplishments, regardless of how little, and invest heavily in the special commitments you bring to the world. Praise your triumphs, of all shapes and sizes, and permit yourself to lounge in the gleam of your achievements.

Besides, perceive that everybody has their own arrangement of assets and gifts, and there is nobody size-fits-all meaning of accomplishment. Embrace your independence and oppose the impulse to contrast yourself with others. All things considered, center around being your best self and amplifying your interesting potential.

As well as praising your assets, challenge yourself to step beyond your usual range of familiarity and investigate new open doors for development and improvement. Propelling yourself past your apparent cutoff points fortifies your current assets as well as develops new ones, growing your collection of abilities and capacities.

At long last, recall that self-acknowledgment is a continuous cycle — an excursion instead of an objective. Be patient and empathetic with yourself as you explore the promising and less promising times of life, and recollect that your value isn't dependent upon outside approval or accomplishment. By commending your assets and embracing your uniqueness, you honor the pith of what your identity is and prepare for a more certain, satisfied, and bona fide life.

Embracing Blemish:

In a world that frequently praises flawlessness, embracing defect can be an extreme demonstration of self-acknowledgment. Blemish is definitely not an indication of shortcoming or disappointment yet rather a characteristic and unavoidable piece of the human experience. By embracing our defects, we free ourselves from the ridiculous guidelines and assumptions that keep us down and figure out how to genuinely adore ourselves.

One of the most vital phases in embracing defect is to relinquish the fantasy of flawlessness — the conviction that we should have everything in perfect order and never commit errors to deserve love and acknowledgment. Actually flawlessness is unreachable and impractical, and taking a stab at it just prompts dissatisfaction, tension, and self-question.

Rather than pursuing flawlessness, center around progress and development. Embrace the possibility of "sufficient" and permit yourself to commit errors, realizing that they are potential open doors for learning and development. Commend your endeavors and achievements, regardless of how blemished they might be, and allow yourself to be human.

One more key part of embracing blemish is developing self-empathy — the capacity to treat ourselves with benevolence, understanding, and pardoning, particularly in snapshots of battle or disappointment. As opposed to castigating ourselves for our missteps or saw deficiencies, practice self-empathy by offering ourselves the very love and backing that we would propose to a dear companion experiencing the same thing.

Besides, perceive that flaw makes us one of a kind and intriguing. Our peculiarities, imperfections, and weaknesses make us human and interface us to others on a more profound level. Embrace your defects as a feature of your character and praise the magnificence and legitimacy they bring to your life.

At long last, recollect that defect isn't an impression of your value or worth personally. Your value is innate and genuine, no matter what your defects or missteps. By embracing blemish and embracing yourself completely and genuinely, you free yourself up to a day to day existence loaded up with realness, satisfaction, and self-acknowledgment.

Setting Reasonable Assumptions:

Setting reasonable assumptions is significant for cultivating self-acknowledgment and building certainty. Time and again, we set unthinkably exclusive requirements for us and castigate ourselves when we definitely miss the mark. By defining reasonable and feasible objectives, we make a pathway to progress that is grounded in self-empathy and mindfulness.

Begin by analyzing your ongoing assumptions and objectives. Is it true or not that they are sensible and feasible, or would they say they depend on unreasonable beliefs or correlations with others? Be straightforward with yourself about what you can possibly achieve given your ongoing conditions, assets, and capacities.

Whenever you have distinguished your objectives, separate them into more modest, reasonable advances. This makes them less overpowering as well as improves your probability of progress. Set explicit, quantifiable, feasible, important, and time-bound (Brilliant) objectives that line up with your qualities and needs.

Be adaptable and ready to change your assumptions on a case by case basis. Life is eccentric, and conditions might change, expecting you to in like manner adjust your objectives and plans. Practice self-empathy and advise yourself that it's OK to recalibrate and correct your assumptions as you explore the high points and low points of life.

Also, praise your advancement and achievements enroute, regardless of how little. Perceive that achievement isn't just about arriving at the end objective yet additionally about the excursion and the development that happens enroute. By recognizing your endeavors and accomplishments, you support your certainty and self-esteem.

At last, recall that self-acknowledgment isn't dependent upon outside accomplishments or honors. Your value is intrinsic and unqualified, whether or not you meet your objectives or not. By setting practical assumptions and embracing yourself completely and genuinely, you make an establishment for unshakeable certainty and internal harmony.

| 4 |

Chapter 4: Stepping Out of Your Comfort Zone

Understanding the Safe place:

The safe place is a mental space where we have a good sense of reassurance, secure, and natural. It's where we work on auto-pilot, liberated from the tension and vulnerability that accompany venturing beyond our laid out schedules and propensities. While the safe place gives a feeling of solidness and consistency, it can likewise be an obstruction to self-awareness and improvement.

At its center, the safe place is an impression of our normal repugnance for hazard and change. It's where we retreat when confronted with new circumstances or difficulties, looking for shelter in the natural and the known. While this nature served our predecessors well in the midst of peril, in the advanced world, it can keep us away from arriving at our maximum capacity.

Venturing beyond our usual ranges of familiarity is fundamental for self-awareness and self-revelation. It's where we face our feelings of dread, push our limits, and uncover stowed away qualities and capacities we never realized we had. By wandering into an unfamiliar area, we grow our viewpoints, expand our points of view, and develop strength and versatility.

Besides, the safe place is definitely not a decent substance but instead a liquid and steadily evolving idea. What might have once been beyond our usual range of familiarity can get comfortable with time and practice, while new difficulties and encounters consistently push the limits of what we see as agreeable.

By understanding the safe place and its part in our lives, we can start to challenge its limits and embrace the open doors for development and change that lie past its limits. Venturing beyond our usual ranges of familiarity might be awkward and testing, however it is where genuine development and self-disclosure happen, pushing us toward an existence of satisfaction, reason, and unshakeable certainty.

Perceiving Restricting Convictions:

Installed inside the safe place are many times a bunch of profoundly instilled restricting convictions that keep us fastened to commonality and keep us from wandering into the unexplored world. These convictions, frequently framed right off the bat throughout everyday life and built up by our encounters, shape our view of ourselves and our general surroundings, directing what we accept is conceivable or unthinkable.

Normal restricting convictions incorporate ideas, for example, "I'm not sufficient," "I'm anxious about disappointment," or "I won't ever succeed." These convictions go about as willful boundaries, obliging our true capacity and keeping us from chasing after our fantasies and desires. They make a restricted focal point through which we view ourselves and the world, sifting through open doors for development and extension.

Perceiving these restricting convictions is the most vital move toward breaking liberated from their grasp and extending our usual ranges of familiarity. It requires thoughtfulness and mindfulness —

looking at the considerations and convictions that emerge when we examine venturing beyond our natural schedules and propensities.

When we become mindful of our restricting convictions, we can start to challenge their legitimacy and supplant them with seriously enabling and steady convictions. This cycle includes scrutinizing the proof supporting these convictions, taking into account elective viewpoints, and reexamining our considerations in a more useful light.

For instance, rather than accepting "I'm not adequate," we can reevaluate it as "I deserve achievement and fit for accomplishing my objectives." As opposed to dreading disappointment, we can embrace it as a chance for development and learning. By testing our restricting convictions and embracing a development outlook, we free ourselves up to additional opportunities and valuable open doors for development.

Additionally, it's critical to perceive that restricting convictions are not realities yet rather translations of reality in view of our previous encounters and discernments. By reexamining our convictions and testing their legitimacy, we can make new brain connections in the cerebrum and develop an outlook that is helpful for development and self-disclosure.

By perceiving and testing our restricting convictions, we prepare for individual change and development of our usual ranges of familiarity. We free ourselves from the requirements of deliberate restrictions and free ourselves up to a universe of vast potential outcomes and valuable open doors for development.

Embracing Dread and Vulnerability:

Dread and vulnerability are regular colleagues on the excursion of venturing beyond our usual ranges of familiarity. They frequently emerge when we examine facing challenges or wandering into the obscure, setting off sensations of tension, uncertainty, and frailty. While our nature might be to keep away from or oppose these awkward feelings, embracing them is fundamental for self-improvement and self-disclosure.

Dread and vulnerability act as signs guiding us to areas of development and extension. They show that we are on the limit of venturing beyond our usual ranges of familiarity and testing ourselves in new and new ways. Instead of review them as obstructions to be survived, we can decide to consider them to be amazing open doors for development and change.

One strong procedure for embracing dread and vulnerability is care — the act of being available and mindful of our viewpoints, sentiments, and sensations without judgment. By developing care, we can notice our feelings of trepidation and vulnerabilities with interest and sympathy, instead of permitting them to control us.

Another procedure is to rethink our view of dread and vulnerability. Rather than seeing them as dangers to our security and security, we can see them as solicitations to fortitude and experience. By reexamining dread as energy and vulnerability as probability, we shift our attitude from one of evasion to one of investigation and interest.

Besides, it's vital to perceive that trepidation and vulnerability are not marks of shortcoming yet rather indications of fortitude and development. Venturing beyond our usual ranges of familiarity requires mental fortitude — the ability to overcome our feelings of trepidation and face challenges in quest for our objectives and dreams.

At long last, taking little, steady strides beyond our usual ranges of familiarity can assist us with building certainty and versatility despite dread and vulnerability. As opposed to endeavoring to handle our greatest apprehensions at the same time, we can begin with more modest, more sensible difficulties and slowly move gradually up to bigger ones.

By embracing dread and vulnerability as essential pieces of the excursion of self-improvement, we develop strength, mental fortitude, and confidence. We figure out how to trust ourselves and our capacities, realizing that we are fit for defeating anything difficulties might emerge. In doing as such, we extend our usual ranges of familiarity and free ourselves up to a universe of vast potential outcomes and valuable open doors for development.

Putting forth Stretch Objectives:

Laying out stretch objectives is a strong technique for extending our usual ranges of familiarity and arriving at new levels of individual and expert development. Not at all like conventional objectives, which are much of the time in light of what we definitely realize we can accomplish, stretch objectives push us past our apparent cutoff points and challenge us to take a stab at significance.

The idea of stretch objectives was advocated by authoritative analyst Edwin Locke, who characterized them as aggressive yet feasible objectives that expect us to expand ourselves past our ongoing capacities. Stretch objectives move us to reach higher, push harder, and accomplish more than we at any point expected.

While putting forth stretch objectives, finding some kind of harmony among desire and feasibility is significant. While stretch objectives ought to be adequately provoking to move us to extend past our usual ranges of familiarity, they ought to likewise be reachable with exertion and responsibility. Putting forth unreasonable objectives can prompt dissatisfaction and demotivation, while laying out attainable stretch objectives can fuel our inspiration and drive our advancement.

Also, stretch objectives ought to be lined up with our qualities, interests, and long haul yearnings. They ought to address significant targets that reverberate with our feeling of direction and vision for what's to come. By interfacing our stretch objectives to our more profound inspirations, we increment our responsibility and commitment to accomplishing them.

As well as putting forth stretch objectives, it's fundamental for break them down into more modest, noteworthy advances that we can take to draw nearer to our targets. This forestalls overpower and gives a guide to accomplishing our objectives methodically.

Moreover, embracing a development outlook is fundamental for seeking after stretch objectives really. A development mentality is the conviction that our capacities and insight can be created through commitment and difficult work, as opposed to being fixed qualities. By taking on a development outlook, we become stronger even with mishaps and more able to embrace difficulties as any open doors for learning and development.

Eventually, laying out stretch objectives is tied in with pushing the limits of what we accept is conceivable and provoking ourselves to arrive at new levels of accomplishment and satisfaction. By embracing the inconvenience and vulnerability that accompany chasing after stretch objectives, we grow our usual ranges of familiarity and open our maximum capacity for significance.

Making a move:

Making a move is the last pivotal move toward getting out of our usual ranges of familiarity and transforming our desires into the real world. While defining objectives and goals is fundamental, it is through activity that we rejuvenate them and make significant change in our lives.

Frequently, the hardest piece of venturing beyond our usual ranges of familiarity is bringing that underlying jump into the unexplored world. We might feel incapacitated by dread, uncertainty, or vulnerability, uncertain of what lies ahead or whether we have the stuff to succeed. Nonetheless, it is at these times of uneasiness and vulnerability that making a move turns out to be generally basic.

One powerful technique for making a move is to separate errands into more modest, more sensible advances. By breaking our objectives into scaled down activities, we make them not so much overpowering but rather more feasible. This approach permits us to zero in on slowly and deliberately, step by step gathering speed and certainty as we progress toward our objectives.

In addition, focusing on activity over perfection is fundamental. Hanging tight for the ideal second or conditions to make a move frequently prompts hesitation and botched open doors. All things considered, embrace the idea of "sufficient" and make a flawed move, realizing that it is smarter to make a defective move than to make no move by any stretch of the imagination.

Another system is to use the force of responsibility and backing. Share your objectives and goals with companions, family, or a coach who can give consolation, direction, and responsibility enroute. Having somebody to applaud you and consider you responsible can have a significant effect in remaining persuaded and focused on making a move.

Besides, develop a development mentality — one that perspectives challenges as any open doors for development and disappointment as a characteristic piece of the growing experience. Embrace misfortunes and obstructions as important growth opportunities that assist you with developing further and smarter on your excursion.

At last, commend your advancement and achievements enroute, regardless of how little. Recognize the boldness and strength it makes to stride beyond your usual range of familiarity and make a move toward your objectives. By praising your successes, you support your certainty and inspiration to keep making a move and seeking after your fantasies.

All in all, making a move is the way to venturing beyond our usual ranges of familiarity and making the existence we want. By embracing inconvenience and vulnerability and taking intentional, reliable activity toward our objectives, we extend our usual ranges of familiarity, open our maximum capacity, and make a day to day existence loaded up with reason, enthusiasm, and satisfaction.

| 5 |

Chapter 5: Taking Action and Building Momentum

The Force of Making a move:

Making a move is the foundation of progress and accomplishment. It is through activity that we transform our fantasies into the real world, our aims into results. While putting forth objectives and imagining achievement are significant initial steps, the predictable and conscious activity moves us forward and carries us nearer to our goals.

One of the main advantages of making a move is that it makes force. Like a snowball moving down a slope, each activity we take expands upon the last, acquiring velocity and energy as it goes. Energy is a strong power that fills our headway and causes accomplishing our objectives to feel more feasible and reachable.

Besides, making a move assists us with conquering idleness — the propensity to stay caught in our ongoing conditions and oppose change. By venturing out, we break liberated from the hold of hesitation and dormancy, picking up speed and energy with each ensuing activity.

One more advantage of making a move is that it gives important input and learning open doors. As we make a move toward our objectives, we realize what works and what doesn't, permitting us to change our methodology and course-right depending on the situation. This iterative course of experimentation is fundamental for development and improvement, assisting us with refining our techniques and draw nearer to our ideal results.

Besides, making a move constructs certainty and self-viability — the faith in our capacity to accomplish our objectives and beat difficulties. Each activity we take supports our confidence in ourselves and our ability to make positive change in our lives. This, thus, propels us to make a further move, making a righteous pattern of progress and accomplishment.

In synopsis, making a move is the impetus for progress and change. It gathers speed, beats idleness, gives significant input, and lifts certainty and self-viability. By embracing the force of activity and focusing on predictable, conscious activity toward our objectives, we release our maximum capacity and make the existence we want.

Beating Delaying:

Delaying is a shared adversary of progress and efficiency, frequently remaining among us and our objectives. It's the propensity to postpone or try not to make a move on errands or objectives, picking rather for momentary joy or solace. Conquering tarrying requires grasping its hidden makes and executing procedures neutralize its belongings.

One of the essential drivers of delaying is dread — anxiety toward disappointment, apprehension about progress, or anxiety toward the unexplored world. At the point when we dawdle, we are frequently keeping away from distress or vulnerability related with making a move. By recognizing and tending to our apprehensions, we can diminish their hold over us and feel more engaged to make a move.

One more typical reason for stalling is hairsplitting — the conviction that our endeavors should be immaculate or wonderful before we can continue. Compulsiveness can prompt loss of motion, as we become overpowered by the anxiety toward committing errors or missing the mark concerning our own unreasonable principles. By embracing defect and embracing an outlook of progress over flawlessness, we can conquer hairsplitting and make a move in spite of our feelings of trepidation.

Besides, hesitation frequently comes from an absence of clearness or bearing. At the point when we are questionable about what moves toward take or how to continue, putting off making a move altogether is simple. By separating errands into more modest, more sensible advances and making an unmistakable strategy, we can diminish overpower and make it simpler to begin.

Also, outside interruptions like virtual entertainment, TV, or different types of diversion can fuel tarrying by giving helpful interruptions from the main job. By limiting interruptions and establishing a favorable climate for concentration and efficiency, we can improve our probability of making a move.

At last, considering ourselves responsible can be a strong counteractant to dawdling. By setting cutoff times, laying out responsibility associations, or openly focusing on our objectives, we make outside strain to finish our goals and conquer lingering.

In outline, defeating lingering requires tending to its hidden causes, like apprehension, compulsiveness, absence of lucidity, and outside interruptions. By carrying out techniques to neutralize these variables and considering ourselves responsible, we can break liberated from the grasp of delaying and make a reliable move toward our objectives.

Developing Consistency:

Consistency is the fuel that supports force and drives long haul achievement. It is the obligation to making a move every day of the week, in any event, when inspiration winds down or snags emerge. Developing consistency requires discipline, commitment, and an eagerness to focus on our objectives over momentary satisfaction.

One of the vital advantages of consistency is that it constructs propensities — the programmed ways of behaving and schedules that shape our regular routines. By reliably making a move toward our objectives, we support brain connections in the cerebrum, making it more straightforward to rehash those ways of behaving from here on out. Over the long run, these ways of behaving become instilled propensities that require less cognizant exertion and resolution to keep up with.

Also, consistency breeds certainty and self-trust. At the point when we reliably finish our responsibilities and make a move toward our objectives, we show to ourselves that we are solid and fit for accomplishing what we set off on a mission to do. This, thusly, supports our certainty and confidence, building up our faith in our capacity to succeed.

Consistency likewise makes a feeling of progress and positive progress. By showing up reliably and gaining steady headway toward our objectives, we gather speed that impels us forward, even notwithstanding mishaps or deterrents. This feeling of progress can be inconceivably spurring, moving us to keep making a move and pushing through difficulties.

Besides, consistency encourages responsibility — both to ourselves and to other people. At the point when we focus on making a move reliably, we consider ourselves responsible to completely finish our expectations, in any event, when it's troublesome or badly designed. Moreover, by imparting our objectives and progress to other people, we welcome outside responsibility and backing, improving our probability of remaining predictable.

At last, consistency is fundamental for building trust and believability with ourselves as well as other people. At the point when we reliably follow through on our commitments and responsibilities, we gain the trust and appreciation of everyone around us, reinforcing our connections and notoriety. Additionally, we construct trust inside ourselves, realizing that we can depend on our own capacities and uprightness to accomplish our objectives.

In rundown, developing consistency is fundamental for supporting energy, building propensities, cultivating certainty, and making long haul progress. By focusing on consistency in our activities and responsibilities, we make a strong starting point for development and progress, engaging us to transform our yearnings into the real world.

Tackling the Force of Propensities:

Propensities are the undetectable draftsmen of our lives, molding our ways of behaving, choices, and eventually, our fates. Outfitting the force of propensities is fundamental for gathering speed and supporting advancement toward our objectives. By understanding how propensities work and deliberately developing positive propensities, we can mechanize activities and make enduring change in our lives.

At their center, propensities are framed through an interaction known as the propensity circle, which comprises of three parts: the signal, the daily schedule, and the prize. The sign triggers a particular way of behaving or schedule, which is trailed by a prize that builds up the propensity circle. By distinguishing the signals and rewards related with our propensities, we can purposefully alter or supplant them to make more sure and useful propensities.

One successful procedure for outfitting the force of propensities is to zero in on cornerstone propensities — little, high-influence propensities that meaningfully affect different aspects of our lives. By distinguishing and focusing on cornerstone propensities, like activity, care, or objective setting, we can make forward movement that spills over into different aspects of our lives.

Additionally, consistency is vital to framing propensities. By reliably rehashing a conduct because of a particular sign and compensating ourselves for doing as such, we build up the propensity circle and make it more programmed over the long haul. This interaction, known as propensity stacking, includes connecting another propensity to a current one, making it more straightforward to coordinate into our day to day schedules.

Moreover, establishing a favorable climate can assist with supporting the development of positive propensities. By eliminating deterrents and interruptions and encircling ourselves with signs that brief wanted ways of behaving, we make it more straightforward to adhere to our propensities and remain focused toward our objectives.

Moreover, it's essential to rehearse self-empathy and persistence while shaping new propensities. Propensities find opportunity to create, and difficulties are a characteristic piece of the interaction. Rather than being deterred by difficulties, view them as any open doors for learning and development, and commit once again to your objectives with restored assurance.

In rundown, outfitting the force of propensities is fundamental for gathering speed and making long haul progress. By understanding the propensity circle, zeroing in on cornerstone propensities, rehearsing consistency, establishing a favorable climate, and developing self-sympathy, we can computerize activities and make enduring change in our lives.

Remaining Inspired:

Keeping up with inspiration is vital for supporting energy and making long haul progress. While making a move and building propensities are fundamental parts of progress, inspiration gives the fuel that keeps us pushing ahead, in any event, when confronted with difficulties or mishaps. Developing and supporting inspiration requires understanding its basic drivers and carrying out systems to keep it alive and flourishing.

One key to remaining spurred is to associate with your basic qualities and reason. At the point when our objectives are lined up with our qualities and interests, we are bound to feel roused and propelled to make a move. Carve out opportunity to consider the reason why your objectives are significant to you and how accomplishing them lines up with your bigger reason throughout everyday life.

One more technique for remaining persuaded is to defined convincing objectives that are explicit, testing, and by and by significant. Objectives that are too obscure or impossible can prompt sensations of overpower or disregard, while objectives that are clear, testing, and actually significant are bound to motivate activity and responsibility.

In addition, separating objectives into more modest, more sensible achievements can cause them to feel more reachable and less overwhelming. Commending your advancement enroute, regardless of how little, can likewise support inspiration and build up your obligation to your objectives.

Furthermore, encircling yourself with strong and empowering individuals can assist with keeping your inspiration levels high. Share your objectives and desires with companions, family, or a coach who can give responsibility, consolation, and backing enroute. Their confidence in your capacities can assist with filling your inspiration and keep you on target when confronted with difficulties.

Moreover, developing a development mentality — the conviction that our capacities and knowledge can be created through commitment and exertion — can assist with supporting inspiration notwithstanding misfortunes or obstructions. Rather than review difficulties as unfavorable deterrents, consider them to be valuable open doors for learning and development, and move toward them with interest and versatility.

In synopsis, remaining roused is fundamental for supporting energy and making long haul progress. By associating with your qualities and reason, defining convincing objectives, separating them into sensible achievements, encircling yourself with strong individuals, and developing a development mentality, you can keep your inspiration levels high and keep gaining ground toward your objectives, even despite difficulties or mishaps.

| 6 |

Conclusion:

Recap of Central issues:

All through this book, we've investigated fundamental standards for opening unshakeable certainty and taking advantage of your internal power. We started by figuring out the idea of certainty and its significant effect on each part of our lives. We dove into the significance of developing a positive mentality, perceiving that our considerations shape our existence and impact our certainty levels.

Besides, we talked about the meaning of embracing self-acknowledgment, recognizing that genuine certainty comes from embracing our assets, blemishes, and uniqueness. We then, at that point, investigated the distress of venturing beyond our usual ranges of familiarity, remembering it as an important stage for development and self-disclosure.

In conclusion, we accentuated the basic job of making a move, for what it's worth through predictable exertion and conscious activity that we harden our certainty and accomplish our objectives. These central issues act as points of support for building unshakeable certainty and opening your inward power.

Reflection on Self-improvement:

As we finish up this excursion, pause for a minute to ponder your very own development and advancement. Consider how you might interpret certainty has extended and how you've applied the standards talked about in this book to your life. Ponder the snapshots of self-revelation and development that have molded your excursion toward unshakeable certainty.

Contemplate the difficulties you've confronted and the deterrents you've survived, perceiving that every difficulty has been a chance for learning and strength. Consider the headway you've made and the objectives you've accomplished, commending your triumphs regardless of how little.

Additionally, think about how your mentality has moved in the meantime. Have you seen a more noteworthy feeling of energy and confidence in your viewpoints and perspectives? How has embracing self-acknowledgment influenced your healthy identity worth and certainty?

Consider the times when you've ventured beyond your usual range of familiarity and embraced the uneasiness of development. What have you found out about yourself in those snapshots of fortitude and weakness? How have they added to your general feeling of certainty and strengthening?

In conclusion, consider the moves you've made to draw nearer to your objectives and dreams. How have these activities built up your certainty and confidence in yourself? What further advances could you at any point take to keep gathering speed and accomplishing your desires?

Reflection is a useful asset for development and mindfulness. Utilize this chance to recognize your advancement, commend your accomplishments, and distinguish regions for additional development and improvement. Recollect that the excursion toward unshakeable certainty is continuous, and each step you take carries you closer to understanding your maximum capacity.

Obligation to Nonstop Improvement:

As you ponder your excursion toward unshakeable certainty, perceive that self-improvement is a deep rooted process. Focus on embracing an outlook of ceaseless improvement, recognizing that there is dependably space to learn, develop, and advance.

Commit to yourself to focus on your self-improvement and put resources into exercises and practices that support your certainty and inward power. This might include understanding books, going to studios, looking for mentorship, or participating in exercises that challenge you to step beyond your usual range of familiarity.

Also, be available to input and productive analysis, perceiving that it offers important bits of knowledge and open doors for development. Embrace difficulties as any open doors for learning and improvement, realizing that every impediment you defeat reinforces your versatility and strengthens your certainty.

Put forth objectives for yourself that move and spur you to arrive at new levels of accomplishment and satisfaction. Separate these objectives into significant stages and focus on taking predictable, purposeful activity toward their achievement.

Most importantly, develop a healthy identity sympathy and thoughtfulness toward yourself as you explore the promising and less promising times of your excursion. Commend your advancement and triumphs, regardless of how little, and be delicate with yourself in snapshots of battle or misfortune.

By focusing on nonstop improvement, you extend your certainty and inward power as well as motivate others to do likewise. Your excursion toward unshakeable certainty is a demonstration of the extraordinary force of development and strength, and by embracing it sincerely, you prepare for a day to day existence loaded up with reason, enthusiasm, and satisfaction.

Support for Flexibility:

In your quest for unshakeable certainty, unavoidable you'll experience difficulties, mishaps, and snapshots of uncertainty. During these times, it's fundamental to develop versatility — the capacity to return from difficulty and keep pushing ahead earnestly and strength.

Advise yourself that misfortunes are not characteristic of disappointment but instead valuable open doors for development and learning. Every deterrent you face presents an opportunity to reinforce your flexibility muscles and develop how you might interpret yourself and your capacities.

Practice self-empathy and generosity toward yourself during troublesome times. Offer yourself inspirational statements and backing, recognizing the fortitude and assurance it takes to deal with difficulties directly.

Look for motivation from other people who have conquered misfortune and made progress in spite of confronting critical impediments. Their accounts act as updates that strength isn't just imaginable however feasible, even notwithstanding apparently unrealistic chances.

Recall that flexibility is an expertise that can be created and reinforced over the long run. By embracing difficulties with a development mentality and keeping an inspirational perspective, you engage yourself to explore life's highs and lows with beauty and versatility.

Most importantly, trust in your capacity to endure and conquer anything that difficulties might come your direction. Have faith in yourself and your ability to endure the hardships of life, realizing that every difficulty carries you one bit nearer to understanding your maximum capacity and carrying on with an existence of unshakeable certainty and inward power.

Source of inspiration:

As you finish up this excursion toward unshakeable certainty and opening your internal power, now is the ideal time to make an interpretation of reflection right into it. Focus on executing the experiences and procedures you've acquired from this book into your everyday existence.

Set explicit, quantifiable objectives that line up with your vision of certainty and self-improvement. Separate these objectives into significant stages and make an arrangement for how you will accomplish them. Consider yourself responsible to your responsibilities and keep tabs on your development enroute.

Search out potential chances to challenge yourself and step beyond your usual range of familiarity. Embrace inconvenience as an indication of development and opportunity, realizing that it is through confronting difficulties that we construct flexibility and certainty.

Encircle yourself with steady and empowering individuals who elevate and motivate you on your excursion. Share your objectives and yearnings with them, and rest on their direction and backing when required.

Practice taking care of oneself and focus on exercises that support your whole self. Develop propensities that help your prosperity and add to your general feeling of certainty and inward harmony.

Most importantly, recollect that certainty isn't an objective however an excursion — an excursion of self-disclosure, development, and strengthening. Embrace the difficulties, commend the triumphs, and confidence in your capacity to make the existence you want.

By making a move and focusing on your development and improvement, you raise yourself as well as rouse others to do likewise. Your excursion toward unshakeable certainty is a demonstration of the boundless possible that exists in every one of us, and by embracing it completely, you become a guide of light and motivation for others to follow.